Kyrie Irving

The incredible story of Kyrie Irving – one of basketball's greatest players!

Table of Contents

Introduction

Thank you for taking the time to pick up this book all about Kyrie Irving!

This book covers the topic of the NBA superstar Kyrie Irving, and how he came to be an NBA champion!

In the following chapters, you will learn all about Kyrie Irving's life and career up to this point. You'll discover stories from his early life, his high school and college days, and also his short time in the NBA.

During his relatively short NBA career, Kyrie has already experienced an incredible amount of success. His journey is an interesting one, and many lessons can be learned from his work ethic and humble attitude.

At the completion of this book, you will have a good understanding Kyrie Irving and his inspiring life and career, as well as what's next for this exciting player!

Once again, thanks for choosing this book, I hope you find it to be interesting and inspiring!

Chapter 1: The Early Life of Kyrie Irving

In 1992, Kyrie Irving was born in Australia to a professional basketball player and his mother, Elizabeth. His father was staying in Australia when Kyrie was born, which naturally meant that Kyrie was to be born there. Despite the fact that he was born in Australia, he has been perceived as raw American talent. This is perhaps because he grew up in the states.

When Kyrie was only two years old, the family brought their extended stay in Australia to an end. They moved back to the United States shortly after. Kyrie, along with his older sister Asia, came back with their mother and father and immediately started their lives in the United States. While things were not all that different from how they were in Australia, they still worked with great vigor to adjust to their new life.

Basketball while Young

From the time that Kyrie was very young, basketball played a huge part in his life. His father was a former basketball star and that was something that his father had always wanted to help his children with. He never pushed them hard to be basketball players; instead, he instilled a love for the game in each of them as he nurtured them by showing them the right way to do things. He wanted to make sure that his children loved the game in the way that he did, but also that they were not being pushed to play it in an organized manner just because that was something that he wanted. He helped them by always playing pickup games with them and showing them the right way to play the game so that they would be able to learn the different aspects of it. He wanted to make sure that they were constantly learning and that they would be able to get the most out of the game.

It was important to Kyrie's father that Kyrie knew not only how to play the game but that he also enjoyed it. His father spent hours upon hours with him when he was young. From the time that Kyrie was very young – as soon as he could walk, in fact – he could often be found on the court with his father.

Mother's Influence

Kyrie's mother, Elizabeth, also had a lot of influence during his early days. She was a mother who was able to help her son with a lot of things, and she wanted the best for him. She loved him, his sister and his father. She was always encouraging of the basketball games that Kyrie's father wanted him to play, and she worked hard to allow her family to know that they were loved by her.

Sadly, when Kyrie was just four years old, only a couple of years after the family had moved back to the states, Elizabeth passed away. She died primarily due to an infection that turned into sepsis. It was unfortunately too late for the family or the doctors to do anything for her. Her passing left a huge void in the family but it did not separate them the way that it does some families. Instead, it brought Kyrie and his father much closer than they might have otherwise been.

Morals Over Playing

One thing that Kyrie's father always wanted him to remember is that it takes a lot of morals and skills to be able to play basketball. Kyrie's father did not have quite the same upbringing as Kyrie and he knew that basketball was going to be his saving grace. Coming from a single mother household with four other siblings and living in the projects while being raised on welfare, Kyrie's father knew that he had to do something to get out. The older Irving pursued a career in basketball.

He always let people know, though, that he was shaped by his upbringing. There were so many people who he knew that had the same type of upbringing, but they were not ever able to get out of the situations that they were in. He knew that he was different because he set his mind to something and always maintained his morals.

3

While Kyrie never had to eat food that was purchased with a welfare check, never worried about his father running off, and didn't have to share a bedroom with four siblings, he has a lot of morals and values that he keeps in his own heart. This is all thanks to his father having to deal with each of these things and it teaching him a lesson. Kyrie is a better person for the way that his father raised him to be morally strong and honorable. He always puts his morals and values far above the game that he plays in order to bring home a paycheck.

High School

Despite the fact that Kyrie had been playing basketball for his whole life, his talents really began to shine when he was in high school. He was a good player and someone who was able to do much more than other people on the court. He had the help of his father on his side but he also had pure talent that was coursing through his veins. All of this contributed to the fact that Kyrie was getting noticed by scouts and people who were hoping to get the best players on their teams. They wanted Kyrie and he knew that.

Kyrie worked very hard to win games and he was always a team player, even when he was in high school. While he was truly the MVP of the team, he made the rest of the team feel like they were just as important as everyone else who was a part of the game. He wanted each and every person to know that they had a part to play and that his skills would not be able to shine in the way that they did if he did not have the help of the other players.

As a high school basketball player, Kyrie made it clear that he was going to be something different in the world of basketball. He was not like the rest of the stale white bread basketball players that so often dominate high school varsity teams.

Mr. Miyagi

Kyrie's talents were harnessed on the court in high school but he really became enthralled with the game when his own personal

Mr. Miyagi, Pyonin, came to help him with his career. Pyonin was a professional coach who was able to help people from simple high school students to the best basketball players. With the urging of his father, Kyrie began studying basketball under Pyonin. He learned everything that he could about the game and that is what allowed him to reach an elite level as he grew older.

There were many things that Pyonin taught him. The coach worked in conjunction with Kyrie's father, who had served as his only one on one coach up to that point. They cultivated a plan to help get Kyrie where he needed to be. Kyrie, unsurprisingly, went above and beyond and was able to make the most out of the things that they did for him. Kyrie's career is thanks to his commitment, his father's desire to help him, and the basketball wizardry of Pyonin.

Chapter 2: Kyrie Irving at Duke

Duke has always had a promising basketball team, and that was not any different when Irving was there. The fact of the matter is that Kyrie Irving helped to make the Duke team even better than what it was. After starting in 2010, Duke started to see a surge in their number of wins compared to the previous year.

Kyrie Irving was on a team not only with the Plumlee brothers but also with Duke veterans who were going to be able to make the year one of the best seasons that the university had ever seen. The combination of the powers of all of the players who were on the team was able to set the school up for a lot of wins. It helped them to be able to get the scores that they needed to eventually be scouted and helped Duke to get the game points that they wanted to be able to set them far above the rest.

The First Year

The first year that Kyrie Irving was at Duke was one of the best seasons that the school has had to date. It was also a time when the team was struggling slightly with the problems caused by some other players.

When the basketball team accepted Kyrie Irving, they knew that they were going to be able to enjoy the benefits that came with having a player like Kyrie. Coach K was especially impressed with Irving's abilities and made sure to always include him with the team activities even when he was just a Freshman at Duke.

The Following Years

It turned out that the great season that Kyrie Irving had when he first got started at Duke was just a precursor for the rest of the seasons that he was going to have there. His college experience allowed him to get better at the game and gave him the option to have really test himself on the court.

Throughout nearly all of Kyrie Irving's years at Duke, he saw success. This was helped by his teammates but was mainly his doing because he was such a strong presence on the court. It was also something that he knew he was only able to do because of the help that he had from his father and from his successful coach in the beginning. Having the backing of Coach K, long regarded as one of NCAA's best basketball coaches, also helped Kyrie get the success that he wanted and that Duke needed to be able to have to win the seasons when he was there.

Getting Scouted

When Kyrie was just a Freshman, the NBA started to take notice of the things that he was doing. While the NBA could not officially scout him when he was just in his first year of college, they were always watching and waiting to see if he was going to be able to make the right move next. They were interested in Kyrie from the first time that they saw him on the court and that made him work even harder to be even better on the court.

After he had been scouted for the first time, the NBA kept coming back. Since Duke is a relatively high profile basketball team, they were there from the beginning but they always kept an eye out for Irving. They recognized that his professional talents went far beyond even what his father was able to do during the time that he was playing professional basketball. Kyrie Irving was a prodigy even when he was in college, and the NBA knew that (and wanted in on the action).

School Priorities

To go along with the values that his father instilled in him, Kyrie always put college first above basketball. He knew that basketball was important but he also knew that it was important that he complete his education before he was able to go anywhere with basketball. This meant that he focused more on his studies than on playing and it also allowed him to have some of the best academic grades of anyone on the team – he was never really in danger of being benched due to his grades, unlike some of the other people who were on the team.

Kyrie knew that he would not be able to play basketball forever. He also knew that he had a chance to get into the NBA but he knew that the chance was relatively slim. He wanted to make sure that he was going to be able to figure out what he was doing after the basketball career was over and after he was unable to continue with the things that he was doing – for that reason, he continued to study hard and to do everything that he needed to get his degree from Duke. Basketball was always on his priority list but school was always higher.

Keeping the Morals

Even when playing for one of the best teams in the nation and being one of the most wanted players in the NBA, Kyrie Irving knew that he had to remember where he came from. It wasn't that he had such a hard upbringing like his father but his father's past helped him to stay humble about what he was doing, too. The morals that his father had taught him stuck, and they were able to help Kyrie figure out that basketball wasn't the only thing in life that mattered.

It was these morals that helped him to be not only a better basketball player but also a better teammate, a better student, and a better person in general. He wanted to make sure that he was always doing the things that were morally right and he made sure to do them every chance that he got. This helped to set him apart when he was in college and it is still helping to set him apart from some of the other basketball players who are a part of the NBA today.

The Teammates

Kyrie is often the most valuable player on the teams that he is a part of. This is something that is familiar to him and something that he knows is a great honor. The one thing that Kyrie always keeps in mind, though, is that he cannot do anything without the help of his teammates. He knows that the teammates are what makes the team and that he needs to work *with* them to continue being one of the best players in the NBA. He knew this even during college and always made sure to point out the help that he was able to receive from the people who he played with.

It was a great honor for Kyrie to be able to get what he needed with the Duke team but it was also something that he felt he needed to honor his teammates with, as well. There were many times when he credited the success that he had not only to his father, his coaches and his mentors in the past, but also to the great support that he received from all of his teammates over the years that he was able to get things done. He couldn't have done it without them.

Going for the NBA

While nearly anyone would be pleased to be offered the opportunity to play in the NBA, Kyrie had to think about it and decide if it was something that he really wanted to be able to do. There were many things that went into his decision and mainly his father's commitment to the sport played a huge part in the decision. There were many different things that Kyrie took into account before making his final decision.

When it came time to be recruited, Kyrie Irving knew what he wanted and what he didn't want. He had the past professional help of his father to guide him, as well as the advice that he was able to take from the mentors in his life. Ultimately, though, Kyrie Irving made the right decision to join the NBA with the team that he felt was working right for him. He has been successful since then.

Chapter 3: Going into the NBA

While the NBA hadn't always been on Kyrie Irving's radar, it quickly became something that he was going to start working for when he was in college. He knew that he was being scouted and this gave him the encouragement that he needed to make sure that he was pushing hard to be the best point guard that he could be. It was something that he knew he was going to have to work hard at if he wanted to continue his career with the NBA and go as far as he could. There were many things that Kyrie did during college, but he made sure that he always had the idea of the NBA in his sights.

The NBA was the right choice and something that Kyrie knew he was going to have to work hard at. It turned out that he was just as successful with the NBA as he had been with all of his other basketball ventures, and has quickly become one of the stars of the NBA during his short career.

Drafting

The year that Kyrie Irving was drafted into the NBA was a year that there were some really poor drafting choices for many teams who desperately needed new talent. There were not many choices for the teams, and many draft picks ended up flopping because the players weren't ready for the NBA.

The only one that truly stood out and was different from the rest of the players that were available during that season was Kyrie Irving. He worked hard at Duke even though he only played 11 total games for the school. The people who recruited him knew that he was going to be among the best and, for that reason, he became one of the top draft picks for that year. He stood way out among the other players, and the coaches for the NBA knew this … they wanted to see him be as successful as possible.

First Season

The first season that Kyrie Irving played in the NBA was similar to the first season that he played in college. He wanted to make sure that he was going to be able to score as much as possible and develop his game further, and for that reason, he worked very hard within the NBA.

Since Irving had played far more games in high school than he had in college, he was more of a high school method player. This was something that his coaches had worried about at the beginning of his NBA career but was also something that they quickly realized was going to help him. He played just like he did in high school which set him far apart from what the other players did. He was just as experienced as they were but he seemed to think differently on the court. He brought a lot of great ideas and new, fresh information to the NBA.

Second Season

Just like when Kyrie Irving was at Duke, his second season was just the beginning of the success that he was going to see. The first season was the foundation, and the second season gave him the chance to start to shine. Similar to how scouts had noticed him while he was playing in college, people began to take notice of him. They saw what a great player he was, how well he did while he was on the court and what he was able to do with the different things that were going on in the NBA at the time. It allowed him the chance to make his talents shine through.

There were many different things that Kyrie Irving did during his second season in the NBA. He adjusted further to the pace of the game, he tried new plays, and he worked to make sure that he was always doing the best job possible.

All Stars

As someone who had only completed their second season with the NBA, Kyrie Irving was able to become an all-star. He was put on an all-star team, and that gave him even more opportunities to be able to get the most out of his NBA career. It also gave him the opportunity to showcase his skills to a larger audience during one of the NBA's biggest weekends.

The Real MVP

In just his third season, Kyrie Irving took home the MVP title for his team. This was a huge honor and something that rarely happens for players in just their third year. He was the MVP and someone who the rest of the teammates would be able to look up to on and off the court.

Just like when he had been the MVP when he was in high school, Kyrie did not let it get to his head. He knew that he wouldn't be able to do it without his teammates and he also knew that they were the ones who had helped him get to that spot. It gave him the chance to show that he was truly a team player and allowed his teammates to feel like they were also a major part of the career that he had created.

Winning Titles

Throughout his career, even in high school, Kyrie Irving has been able to win a lot of titles for the teams that he has played with. This is no different in the NBA. With the new addition of LeBron James and Kyrie Irving, the Cavaliers were able to achieve championship glory in the 2015/2016 season.

The team that he plays for, the Cavaliers, were able to take home one of the first sporting titles that their city has seen in decades. While it cannot be all completely credited to Kyrie, he had a very large contribution to their success. Kyrie has now played far more games than he did in college and he plans to lead his team to even more titles in the future. He is not going to stop anytime soon and plans to continue seeing a lot of success in the NBA.

Chapter 4: Problems Kyrie Irving Has Overcome

Everyone has problems in their lives, and NBA stars are certainly not immune to these. Kyrie Irving is not an exception to the rule. He has had many issues and challenges that he has been able to overcome. These have been in both his personal life and also in his professional life which has made things harder for him. Because he was able to overcome so much in each of these phases of his life, he has become a very confident and determined young man.

Move to America

The first of many trials that Kyrie would have to go through in his life was moving back to the United States. Even though he was still young when he made the move, it was something that he had to go through and something that he needed to adjust to. It was somewhat difficult for him to have to adjust to living in a new country with new people and even new customs.

Despite the fact that Australia isn't that different from the United States, it was still something that Kyrie Irving needed to handle at a young age. His parents were committed to making sure that both Kyrie and his sister, Asia, were comfortable in their new home and the country that they were going to be living in. They did everything that they could to make them happy and to give them the best opportunities that they could, even when they were struggling on their own at times.

Loss of His Mother

Perhaps one of the worst things that happened to Kyrie was the loss of his mother. This is not something that many people have to go through especially when they are so young. Kyrie was only four when he lost his mom so he doesn't have much recollection of her, but he certainly remembers the painful things that he had to endure when he was older as a result of not having a mother. While his father did a great job of raising him, it was nearly impossible for him to try to replace what a mother could have been able to do for Kyrie.

The loss of his mother had such a huge impact on Kyrie. He credits her death to his success. While it was something painful that he and his father both had to go through, it was also something that brought them much closer together. They would probably not have had the time to bond in the way that they did if his mother were still alive. This challenge ended up being worth a lot to Kyrie because he was able to create a connection to his father through the grief that they both felt.

High School Athletics

In New Jersey, high school basketball is taken very seriously. People take it almost as seriously as they take the college and professional sports in the area. This is something that puts a lot of pressure on kids who are playing basketball in high school in New Jersey. It isn't just something that they can do for fun – the sport is taken so seriously that they are often under a lot of pressure to succeed and help their teams win.

It was sometimes hard for him to be able to keep up, but with the help of his former professional father and the coach that they hired, he was able to handle the pressure.

Games in College

During his college career, Kyrie Irving only played 11 games due to injury. This was something that was upsetting to him, but ultimately it did not hinder his NBA career. The obvious stress of not being able to play at such a crucial time made him anxious about his NBA career prospects. However, Kyrie managed to practice as much as he could, even though he wasn't game-ready.

Doubts from NBA

The NBA was interested in Irving, but they were seriously concerned because he had played so few games while he was in college. He was a high school player in the truest sense, and it concerned all of the teams. Kyrie was worried that he would not get picked for any team. He continued to work hard on his basketball skills and tried to make sure that he was going to be just as professional as the other players.

Despite the doubts that many of the NBA professionals had, Kyrie still showed off the skills that he had and wanted to make sure that the NBA saw that he was great at what he did. Even though he did not have a lot of college experience under his belt, he knew that he could bring a lot of value to the team that he was to be a part of.

Picked Up by Cavaliers

The Cavaliers picked Kyrie up. This was a great team out of Cleveland that had a lot of good players and a great coach. The biggest problem with the Cavaliers, though, was that they were a team from Cleveland. The city had not won any major championship in over 20 years, and there was no indication that the city was going to win anything anytime soon. While Kyrie was excited just to be *in* the NBA, he knew that he was going to have to work hard to be able to bring the Cavaliers to a championship.

After some hard work from Kyrie and the acquisition of LeBron James and Kevin Love, the Cavaliers were able to bring home the championship. This was not only the first time in a long time for the basketball team, but it was also the first time in a long time for any major sports team in the city. It allowed them to break a city "curse" and gave them the motivation that they needed, as a team, to come back even better the following season.

Playing with Idols

Kyrie was asked to play on an all star team with people who had been his idols. This was a great opportunity for him, but it also posed some major problems that he had to deal with. He was disappointed after he was done playing because he had to go back to regular mundane playing. He wanted to continue playing with all stars, but he knew that he would have to wait.

International Sensation

Kyrie Irving never expected to be an international player and someone who was going to be a household name around the world, but he was able to do so after he played in his first all-star game. He wanted to make sure that he was going to be known and this is something that he worked hard at.

Chapter 5: Most Memorable Moments for Kyrie

During his time in the NBA, Kyrie Irving has seen a great deal of success. He has helped to bring the Cavaliers a championship, and he has been able to provide them with the stability that they need to be able to continue securing the big wins in the future. It has given him the chance to make a name for himself and also make a name for the team that he plays with.

Kyrie has already had many memorable moments in his short basketball, and is already viewed as one the the league's elite players.

High School Games

Before being brought into Cleveland as an NBA player, Kyrie Irving had a great career as one of the best high school players in New Jersey. This is a state where basketball at the high school level is taken almost as seriously as a professional sport, so it was a huge deal when Kyrie was named as one of the best. He was able to lead his team to a lot of victories while he was playing in high school and that set up the rest of his career.

He consistently stood out as one of the MVPs on his high school team. He enjoyed playing basketball, though, and for him, it was about so much more than winning. He wanted to make sure that he was doing his best and that he was able to get the most out of the sport so that he could continue with it and, hopefully, one day make it a part of his career.

Leading Duke

After graduating high school and being accepted to Duke as a basketball player, Kyrie Irving was able to join the team and have a significant impact. However, he was hindered by a foot injury that would just not get better until he was almost done with college. This prevented him from playing in a lot of games, but he was able to still do a lot with the team. It allowed him to see another side of basketball – the logistics that did not have a lot to do with actually playing.

Despite the fact that Kyrie was not able to play in a lot of games, he still helped Duke do well that season. They made it to the championship, but ultimately lost.

Being Chosen

Just the fact that Kyrie Irving was chosen to play in the NBA was a huge deal and a career-defining moment. Even though he had been on the team with Duke and had done a great job playing the games that he *did* play, he was nowhere near as experienced as many of the other players in the draft. The NBA saw potential in him though, and the Cavaliers selected him in the first round.

The Cavaliers saw that he had a lot of success in high school. They also took into account where he went to high school – New Jersey – and the basketball scene that was there for high school players. They knew that even though he was not a huge college player, his experiences with extremely competitive high school basketball were going to help him to be able to play in the NBA. They knew that he was the right pick and took a gamble on him. It worked out.

Filling Big Shoes

One season before Kyrie Irving started with the Cavaliers, LeBron James had left the team. This was someone who had been one of Kyrie's idols, and he never thought that he would, essentially, have the chance to take his place on the Cavaliers team. It was something that he knew was going to be a big deal and something that he had to do. He had very big shoes that he was going to have to fill with LeBron James, ' and he tried his best to make sure that he was doing his best – he was successful and has quickly become just as much of a legend in Cleveland as James.

Shortly after Kyrie joined the team, LeBron returned to the Cavaliers. His power combined with everything that Kyrie was good at allowed the team to be able to win nearly every game that they played. Kyrie was also particularly excited when LeBron James came back because that was one of his idols. He was going to have a chance to be able to play basketball with someone who he had looked up to for many years. He knew that they were going to be a team that was unbeatable with the combined experience that they had.

Pepsi Commercials

One of the things that has set Kyrie Irving apart from others his age and with his experience is the fact that he has been cast in a series of commercials for Pepsi. This is usually reserved for players who have been playing for many years and are a household name (like LeBron). Kyrie has only been on the scene for a few years, but he is popular enough to be in a commercial. It is something that has set him apart in a different way than his abilities that he has on the court.

The series of 'Uncle Drew' commercials have gone viral worldwide, only increasing Kyrie's fame further.

Big Points

Kyrie has scored quite a few points in his career with the NBA. Since it has been such a short career, it would be hard to say that he has any records. It is easy to see, though, that if he continues to play as he does, he will smash quite a few records before he's finished.

The Championship

The games that changed everything for Kyrie was the championship series against the Golden State Warriors. While he was not the only person who was able to bring the team success in the series, he had a lot to do with the success that the team saw. He not only played hard on his own but he also propelled his teammates to be able to do the same thing. He knew that they were working hard and that he had to work hard, too. He also knew that he was a great motivator and he helped them to see that they could be successful and win the games.

The championship was a career defining moment for everyone on the team, but especially for Irving at such a young age. The Cleveland Cavaliers team is on track to win even more championships with the duo of Kyrie Irving and LeBron James.

Chapter 6: What's Next for Kyrie?

Kyrie Irving has had so much success already in the short career that he has had. He has had so much success, in fact, that it is somewhat hard to believe that he has only been in the NBA for such a short time.

Where do you go though, once you have already won a championship? For Kyrie, the answer is work even harder at becoming the best he can be, both on and off the court.

Training

The time that Kyrie has off between seasons is going to be spent training. While there is, obviously, a time for him to train in the right way, he wants to make sure that he is going to be able to train on his own. He has had a lot of injuries in the time that he has been playing basketball – particularly with his foot. He wants to make sure that he can stay injury free, and enjoy a long and healthy career.

Off Time

During the offseason, Kyrie usually takes some time for himself. He did this even in college, and he knows that it is important to do so that he does not get burnt out.

During the offseason, Kyrie often goes to Australia where he holds dual citizenship. It gives him the chance to be able to go back to his roots and relax.

Around the World

Along with the fact that Kyrie goes to Australia often, he also visits other countries around the world. He enjoys traveling and does it often while he is taking time off. Even though he does not have a very long offseason, he tries to make the most of the time he has

Kyrie is quickly becoming an international sensation. His name is known around the world, and his fame is growing every day. He has endorsements from companies in many different countries, and continues to grow his personal brand.

Moving Teams

There is not a large chance that Kyrie will be moving from the Cavaliers. The team likes him and sees him as one of the best things that have happened to them since they signed LeBron James. They also know that the two work well together and that they will be able to bring all of the success that the team has hoped for.

MVP Status

There has been a lot of talk of MVP in the NBA for Kyrie Irving. This is nearly unheard of for someone who is so young and has had such a short NBA career, but it is something that could happen if Kyrie keeps performing in the way that he is doing. The team could make him the MVP which could put more pressure on him and allow him to perform even better. There is a chance of this and, if it happens, it would be one of the record-breaking things that Kyrie would have done in his NBA career.

Winning Championships

No matter what happens in his career or outside of it, Kyrie Irving plans to continue to win many more championships.

There is a lot of basketball in Kyrie's future. He knows that he will need to play hard, lead his team, and work towards many more championships!

Conclusion

Thanks again for taking the time to read this book!

You should now have a good understanding of Kyrie Irving and his inspiring journey to NBA success!

If you enjoyed this book, please take the time to leave me a review on Amazon. I appreciate your honest feedback, and it helps me to continue producing high-quality books.

CPSIA information can be obtained
at www.ICGtesting.com
Printed in the USA
BVHW041438110719
553202BV00011B/611/P